WARRIORS!
SILENT SOLDIERS

Thanks to the creative team:
Senior Editor: Alice Peebles
Design: www.collaborate.agency
Consultant: John Haywood

Hungry Tomato™
A division of Lerner Publishing Group, Inc.
241 First Avenue North
Minneapolis, MN 55401 USA

For reading levels and more information, look up this title at www.lernerbooks.com.

Main body text set in Bell MT.
Typeface provided by Monotype.

Library of Congress Cataloging-in-Publication Data

The Cataloging-in-Publication Data for *Silent Solders* is on file at the Library of Congress.

ISBN 978-1-4677-9356-8 (lib. bdg.)
ISBN 978-1-4677-9603-3 (pbk.)
ISBN 978-1-4677-9604-0 (EB pdf)

Manufactured in the United States of America
1 – VP – 12/31/15

WARRIORS!
SILENT SOLDIERS

by Catherine Chambers
Illustrated by Jason Juta

HUNGRY TOMATO.

CONTENTS

INTRODUCING SPEED AND STEALTH

Most fighting forces aim to trick the enemy and launch a surprise attack. This basic tactic has not changed for thousands of years all over the world. From small fighting units to great armies, stealth and speed have achieved these aims. Some of the most effective stealth warriors are featured in this book.

WHAT IS STEALTH?

Stealth begins with knowing the enemy. Spies secretly slip into the enemy's world to find out its plan of attack, the size and makeup of its force, and its weaponry. Does it have a strong cavalry? Are its forces equipped for all conditions? Are they well organized and led? Do they have enough food and water? Spies use stealth just to get into the enemy's camp to find these things out! With this information, their own forces can plan their own tactics.

Stealth means silence. The best stealth warriors approach without making a sound or disturbing the undergrowth around them. They know how to signal to each other without giving away their position. Stealth warriors use the terrain to hide and ambush the enemy, and they adopt camouflage to sink unseen into the background before they approach and strike.

Successful stealth warriors use many types of terrain to their advantage. They can climb rock faces to watch the enemy approaching along a valley. Or they can cut their way through thick forests and cross rapid rivers. They ambush the foe, who cannot pursue them over these natural obstacles. Stealth exploits the heat of a blistering hot day, the chill of an icy winter, the dark of night, and the uncertainty of twilight. All these factors can lead to victory.

What is Speed?

Speed is the force of a warrior's or army's approach. This can begin from far away, building up fear in the waiting enemy. It can be a barrage of fire or a shower of arrows, seemingly shot from nowhere. Or it can be close and sudden, springing a surprise on an enemy camp or troops trapped in a dead end with no means of escape. Speed means always holding the initiative, so the enemy has no time to carry out its own plans.

Modern stealth helicopters attack swiftly from many angles. They launch from assault ships or small patches of ground. They have special noise-reduction technology and use silent communication systems.

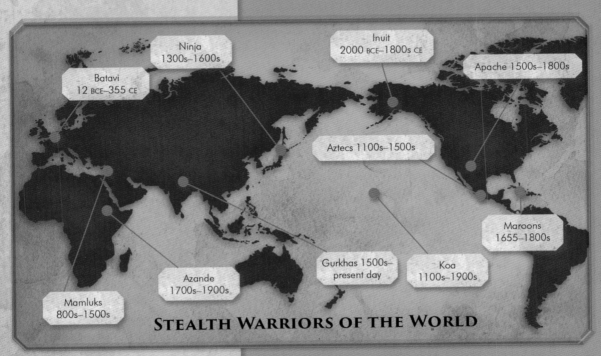

Ninja 1300s–1600s

Inuit 2000 BCE–1800s CE

Apache 1500s–1800s

Batavi 12 BCE–355 CE

Aztecs 1100s–1500s

Maroons 1655–1800s

Gurkhas 1500s–present day

Koa 1100s–1900s

Azande 1700s–1900s

Mamluks 800s–1500s

STEALTH WARRIORS OF THE WORLD

FATAL ATTACKS

Emperor Claudius sent the Batavi to invade Britain in 43 CE. Batavi cavalry crossed the seemingly impassable River Medway, south of London. This pushed the terrified Britons northward.

LETHAL WEAPONS

Batavi cavalry and infantry struck with the Roman *gladius* (sword) and *pilum* (javelin). They even bashed with the central rounded bosses of their shields. They were feared masters of hand-to-hand combat.

TOP TRAINING

Batavi were trained from boyhood to fight with knives, spears, and swords—and with no weapons at all. The Batavi's unique skill was in guiding horses across foaming water, using them as rafts to carry their weapons.

FEROCIOUS FACTS

● Batavi gouged and slashed their enemies' faces.

● Julius Caesar called them "savage and barbarous."

● The Romans saw the Batavi as a valuable resource to be used only in warfare.

BOLD BATAVI

Batavi shock troops fought for the Roman army in the toughest conditions. They formed the Emperor's bodyguard, too. This Germanic tribe came from a wild river island. Their harsh homeland terrain helped them develop the skills and strength to swim across raging torrents in full armor, with weapons and horses. Once across, their units of 500 to 1,000 soldiers pushed back or slaughtered enemy troops on the other side. Their Roman discipline kept the Batavi in close formation. This, coupled with their speed and surprise tactics, gained victories from the area of modern-day Germany to the British Isles.

WHERE
From modern-day Holland to lands in the Roman Empire

WHEN
About 12 BCE–355 CE

ROMAN JAVELIN

- Hard, penetrating barbed tip

- Long iron shank (neck), about 2 ft (60 cm) long

- Overall length 6.5 ft (2 m)

GHOSTLY NINJA

WHERE
Japan

WHEN
1300s–1600s, with
influence up to
the 1800s

Ninja warriors acted as professional spies, saboteurs, and assassins for Japan's warlords. They often practiced deception to work as servants for the enemy. Ninja traveled in bands, slipping silently away from their homes, which had false walls and secret escape passages. They concealed their movements among the shadows, wore air-filled skin pouches to cross raging rivers, and scaled walls using hooks. Ninja were masters of mayhem in both attack and defense. They threw smoke bombs or explosives and sharp metal weapons. In close combat, ninja wielded deadly spikes hidden in the palms of their hands.

Shuriken (throwing star)

- Thin blades with sharpened tips
- Central hole to aid weapon's flight
- Number of points varied from about three to eight
- Metal recycled from everyday items

FATAL ATTACKS

In 1638, the *daimyo* (feudal lord) Matsukuru Shigeharu brutally crushed the peasant Shamabara Rebellion. The peasants were besieged in Hara Castle, and the daimyo's ninja nimbly scaled the walls and attacked.

LETHAL WEAPONS

Ninja were expert archers and swordsmen. They scattered pointed metal caltrops on the ground to wound enemies' feet and flung *shuriken*, or spiked metal stars. They sprayed poisoned water from bamboo pistols.

TOP TRAINING

There were 25 schools for training young ninja in physical and mental toughness, and above all, stealth. They learned how to hide, use weapons, and even hold their breath to feign death.

FEROCIOUS FACTS

- Ninja made their own killer explosives and poisons.
- They escaped from attackers by throwing frogs and poisonous snakes.
- They set fire to enemy gunpowder, weapons, and food stores.

11

FATAL ATTACKS

In 1879, the husband of Gouyen, a Chiricahua Apache, was killed and scalped by a Comanche chief. She used stealth to lure him away, kill him with his own knife, and escape on his horse.

LETHAL WEAPONS

The Chiricahua made clubs from buffalo jawbones with the sharp teeth in place, fixing them to strong, hardwood handles. They added turkey and buzzard feathers to arrows to ensure the smoothest flight. In the 1800s, rifles gave them greater range.

TOP TRAINING

Small children were taught to dance with silent footsteps to learn stealth. They hunted with their fathers to learn skills in stalking, ambush, weaponry, and communicating with animal calls and smoke.

FEROCIOUS FACTS

● Chiricahua Apache set ablaze army and miners' camps and homesteads.

● They could survive longer in rough territory than their enemies by drinking water stored in the barrel cactus and locating hidden food stores.

APACHE SHOCK

Chiricahua Apache raided in bands to take cattle, horses and guns—all needed for their survival. Early on they used a deep knowledge of their landscape and ancient hunting methods against hostile tribes. From the 1800s they needed these skills to fight the Mexican and United States armies, who were confining them in reservations. Chiricahua lured soldiers high up into difficult terrain, then picked them off with rifles, bows and arrows, tomahawks, and clubs. They could run for miles without food or water and avoided leaving tracks on soft earth. Reaching their target, Chiricahua used the calls of wild animals to band together and strike.

WHERE
Southwestern USA and northern Mexico

WHEN
Active in the region about 1500s–1800s

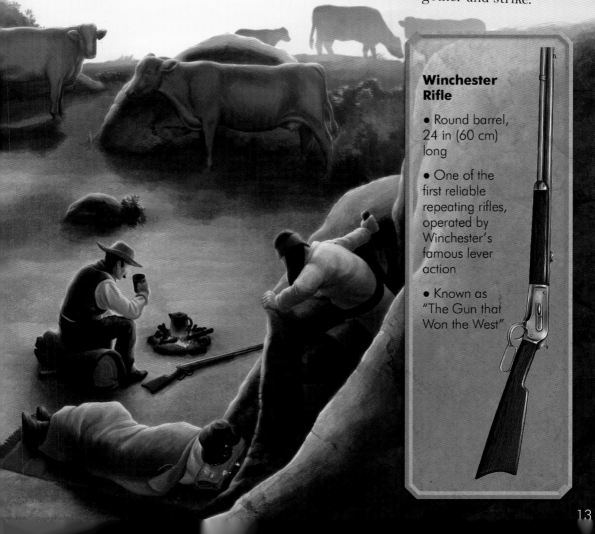

Winchester Rifle

- Round barrel, 24 in (60 cm) long

- One of the first reliable repeating rifles, operated by Winchester's famous lever action

- Known as "The Gun that Won the West"

MYSTERIOUS MAMLUKS

WHERE
Eurasian steppe grasslands

WHEN
800s–1500s, with influence up to 1800s

Mamluk soldiers were enslaved in boyhood by the Arab Abbasid Empire, which covered modern Iraq, Iran, and western Asia. After training, they became free and were a powerful cavalry serving Abbasid rulers. By 1250 Mamluks had begun to carve out their own empire in Egypt and Syria. Royal Mamluks were an elite section guarding their leader. Their *furusiyya* code taught them loyalty, secrecy, martial arts, and speed on horseback. Through their excellent spy networks, Mamluks knew where to ambush and surprise their enemy. Generals used this inside knowledge to position their elite soldiers, ready to strike.

Kilij (saber)

• Curved blade, length about 2 ft (60 cm)

• Blade's curve more pronounced from midpoint to tip, with a double-edged end for extra cutting power

FATAL ATTACKS

Sultan Baybars (1223–1277) secretly gathered his Mamluk troops from afar to strike enemy Mediterranean ports. He famously laid siege to the ancient port of Arsuf in 1265, outwitting European Franks and their Mongol allies.

LETHAL WEAPONS

Mamluks fought with the best *kilij* (sabers), bows and arrows, spears, maces, swords, and later, guns. They also wielded the *tabarzin*, or horseman's axe, which had a steel, crescent-shaped, single or double blade.

TOP TRAINING

Young slave boys were first schooled in Islam, then trained as top horsemen, wrestlers, archers, swordsmen, and javelin throwers. Chess classes helped them to learn battle tactics.

FEROCIOUS FACTS

- Spies sent information via linked "post offices," where fast horses and pigeons waited to carry messages swiftly onward.
- Mamluks burst suddenly into view on their horses, firing arrows tipped with explosive Greek fire.

FATAL ATTACKS

Aztec scouts tried to murder the Spanish military leader Hernán Cortés at a feast. Two Owl assassins slipped poisoned sweet potatoes and tortillas in front of him. But he did not eat them.

LETHAL WEAPONS

Aztec warriors used slings, bows and hefty wooden swords embedded with shards of obsidian, a volcanic glass. Spears, ending in long blades made of flints, were whipped into action with an *atlatl*. This spear thrower unleashed the weapons with maximum speed and force.

TOP TRAINING

Aztec boys began training when they hunted with their fathers. They then entered the *telpochcalli*, or House of Youth, to learn fighting skills. *Cuicacalli*, or military school, taught them their role in the army.

FEROCIOUS FACTS

● To become an Eagle, an Aztec soldier had to capture at least four enemies for sacrificing to the gods.

● Stealth warriors attacked rival states just to capture their citizens so they could be sacrificed to Aztec gods.

SILENT AZTEC SCOUTS

Stealth warriors were the top troops of the Aztec Empire's vast army. They struck quietly in bands or as task forces ahead of up to 200,000 infantry, taking vast amounts of territory and tribute. In uniforms of fearsome creatures, such as jaguars and eagles, Aztec warriors silently scouted their enemy. With the intelligence they gained, they planned their shock attacks. Jaguar and Eagle scouts used excellent close-combat skills and wielded clubs studded with sharp flints that slashed their opponents. However, from 1519, their skills were no match for the cavalry and firearms of the Spanish conquerors of their empire.

WHERE
Central Mexico

WHEN
1100s–1500s

Macuahuitl (wooden sword)

• Overall length from 3 ft (90 cm) to human height

• Embedded shards of obsidian (volcanic glass) or flint, sharp enough to decapitate a man

• One- or two-handed grip

• Carved from oak

GRITTY GURKHAS

WHERE
Nepal

WHEN
1550s–
present day

The Gurkhas' knowledge of their terrain and their discipline, stealth, courage, and use of intelligence are fearsome. In the 1770s, Prithvi Narayan Shah used these very skills to expand his town into the powerful city-state of Gorkha. By day or night, Gurkhas could charge through thick forest, climb steep cliffs, and run along goat paths no wider than two hands. They stalked enemy troops, worked out opponents' movements, and picked off stragglers. Gurkhas dodged rifle fire, then thrust bayonets and long knives into the enemy. All these qualities led the British Army to enlist them in 1815.

Khukuri

● 12-in (30-cm) forward-curving blade, angled toward the opponent

● Overall length about 18 in (45 cm)

● Handle made of hardwood or buffalo horn

● Flared butt for a better grip

FATAL ATTACKS

At the Battle of Gallipoli in modern Turkey in 1915, scouts from the 6th Gurkha Rifles swiftly scaled a cliff toward Turkish fire. The Gurkhas killed 2,000 soldiers and captured the cliff, which was then renamed Gurkha Bluff.

LETHAL WEAPONS

Gurkhas fought with rifles and their traditional knife, the *khukuri*. Its blade curves from the hilt, weighing it down for an easy, swift, chopping movement.

TOP TRAINING

Gurkha boys trained by running at an even pace up steep crags and along narrow passes. Gurkhas practicing for selection into the British Army ran uphill with baskets of rocks on their backs.

FEROCIOUS FACTS

• Gurkhas could kill and cut off a head with just a single swipe of the khukuri.

• Their terrifying battle cry is *"Ayo Gurkhali!"* or "The Gurkhas are coming!"

FATAL ATTACKS

Inuit elders tell ancient tales of famous attacks by bands of up to 50 men, led by a Great Warrior. Their deadliest weapon was a strong recurve bow made of bone.

LETHAL WEAPONS

Inuit struck with harpoons and bows and arrows. In close combat they used bone knives for slicing at combatants, until they traded with Europeans for steel blades. Inuit fired European guns from the 1770s.

TOP TRAINING

Long hunting treks prepared boys for days of walking toward their enemy. They learned how to shoot and throw harpoons and *bolas*, bone weights attached to strings of sinew to entangle animals' legs.

FEROCIOUS FACTS

● Inuit scouts blocked a camp and kashim's exits, leaving just one. At this one exit, scouts attacked all those fleeing through it.

● They often let one enemy live so that he could terrify others with tales of his ordeal.

ALASKAN INUIT ATTACK

Inuit defended their hunting grounds and trade routes with stealth, ambush, and flames. Their warriors struck mostly at night, waiting for their enemies to gather for a meal or festival. Inuit made armor out of small pieces of bone and ivory. This also camouflaged them in the snow. They silently approached the camp or the *kashim*, a village's community building. Then they threw flames inside the building, killing fleeing victims. In early times, Inuit launched these strikes against other feuding villages and tribes. By the 1700s Europeans in the region could be targeted.

WHERE
Alaska

WHEN
About 2000 BCE–
1800s CE

Cable-Backed Bow

• Bow made of three or four antlers, or pieced from driftwood or baleen

• Sinew cable to reinforce the bow, wrapped and tied on with highly skilled knots

• Bone or stone arrow point

DEADLY AZANDE

WHEN

1700s–early 1900s

These fast, deadly warriors expanded their territory and fought Arab traders and European colonialists. In small skirmishes, Azande used stealth tactics and their knowledge of the vast equatorial forest around them to ambush and strike. They stalked their enemy, sometimes firing arrows and spears from long distances. Or they stole up on them, baring sharpened teeth. Then they threw *kpinga* knives that were stored behind large wicker shields and stormed in with sickle-shaped *makraka* blades. In larger battles, a fearsome central column of warriors advanced quickly, with wings that surrounded the enemy.

Kpinga (three-bladed throwing knife)

- Iron blades, each one a different shape and each projecting at a different angle

- Overall length about 22 in (55 cm)

- Small handle made of plant fiber

FATAL ATTACKS

King Gbudwe (1870–1905) united the Zande kingdom, creating a large, disciplined army. At the Battle of Birikiwe in 1898, it chased off Arab Mahdists from the north, throwing spears into their stockade.

LETHAL WEAPONS

The Azande's strong 4-ft (1.2-m) bow was strung with sinew. Its long cane arrows were tipped with iron. The *makrigga* (spear) ripped out flesh and organs with its hooked iron spearhead.

TOP TRAINING

Young Azande practiced wrestling and learned stealth, weaponry, and the use of poisons through hunting. New warriors were given a shield with a unique pattern that made them easily identifiable in battle.

FEARSOME FACTS

● Azande tipped their arrows with a red powder poison made from *benge*, a creeper plant. It took three agonizing hours to kill the victim.

● Their war cry was "*Nyam-nyam!*," meaning "Great eaters!," to scare foes with the threat of cannibalism.

23

FATAL ATTACKS

King Kahekili of Maui (1765–1790) knew that his rival, King Kalani'opu'u, was about to invade his island. So Kahekili hid his troops in the sand dunes, ambushing and then killing the invaders.

LETHAL WEAPONS

The koa tree provided wood for weapons such as the 15-ft (4.5-m) *laumeki*, a barbed spear, as well as daggers, knuckle-dusters, clubs, and throwing axes. Longer-range weapons included slings and, from the 1790s, European cannon.

TOP TRAINING

Sons of chiefs and soldiers of important rank trained in martial arts. They practiced with dancelike movements called *ha'a koa*. As adults, they kept their skills sharp by taking part in tournaments.

FEROCIOUS FACTS

● Koa shaved and oiled their bodies so that the foe could not hold on to them in close combat.

● A chief savagely punished his own soldiers. A guard who fell asleep might have his head chopped off.

HAWAII'S HORROR KOA

Koa stealth troops fought for the Hawaiian Islands' chieftains. These leaders attacked each other regularly until King Kamehameha I (1758-1819) united seven of them. Koa were super-fit elite troops who used the secret art of Lua to overcome their enemy. This included battle tactics, lifting very heavy weights, bone-breaking, and other martial arts. The islands' chieftains, advised by mystical priests, were masters of shock tactics. A campaign might begin with hidden soldiers showering arrows, slingshot, and spears from a great height. Then armed infantry closed in, while Koa pounced, kicking, punching, throwing, and finally killing their victims.

WHERE
Hawaiian Islands

WHEN
About 1100s–1900s

War Club

- Solid koa wood

- Edged with sharks' teeth, tied on with strong bark fiber

- Overall length about 15 in (38 cm)

HIDDEN MOUNTAIN MAROONS

WHERE
Mountains of
Jamaica

WHEN
1655–1800s

In 1655 British soldiers took Jamaica from its Spanish rulers and let their plantation slaves escape to the forested mountains. Here, this hidden community became guerrilla fighters, the Maroons—and the British began to fear them. They learned the terrain and used it well. In disciplined units they gathered information, often from slaves still working on the plantations. Then, in camouflage and often at night, the Maroons descended to the plantations to take on British troops. With screams, drumbeats, and deafening horns, they attacked with arrows, spears, machetes, and, later, rifle fire. They killed their foes, set the plantations ablaze, and released more slaves.

Machete

Broad chopping and hacking blade, up to 18 in (45 cm) long, for cutting cane on sugar plantations

GREAT BATTLES

During the Second Maroon War in 1795, 300 Maroons held off 4,500 British troops and volunteers for five months. The Maroons had made peace in 1739 but had not forgotten their military skills.

TOP TACTICS

Maroons adapted farming tools for warfare, so machetes became cutlasses. They took their victims' swords and rifles. They used conch shells and side-blown cow horns as tools of communication, passing messages by blowing on them.

TOP TRAINING

Boys and girls were trained to find the best lookout posts and ambush points, especially in ravines. They learned how to disguise themselves as bushes or trees, shifting forward, then striking.

FEROCIOUS FACTS

• Maroons used the secret powers of Obeah spirits to scare the enemy.

• They seemed to disappear behind waterfalls, but in reality they slipped through cracks in the rock behind the sheet of water.

27

BATTLES OF SPEED AND STEALTH

STORMING BATAVI

In about 83 CE the Roman General Agricola ordered four battalions of Batavi to attack the fierce tribes in the area that is now Scotland. This is called the Battle of Mons Graupius. Under General Quintus Petilius Cerialis, the Batavi engaged their enemy in hand-to-hand combat. They struck the Caledonian tribesmen with the bosses of their shields, stabbed them in the head, and pushed them back. Other Roman battalions, encouraged by the Batavi, followed behind.

COMET POWER

King Kamehameha the Great (1758–1819) used infantry and Koa stealth warriors to unite seven Hawaiian islands by 1810. He also used his spiritual power. This chief's son had been born when Halley's Comet crossed the skies, and it was believed that this gave him the strength to conquer other chiefs. His opponents were so tough that it took him 15 years to defeat them. His greatest victory was the Battle of Nu'anu Pali in 1795.

White on White

Between 1100 and 1300, early Alaskan Inuit people called the Thule moved across the Canadian Arctic. They spread into northern Greenland and used the terrain and their traditional stealth tactics to attack Viking settlements. One of their most successful tactics was covering their kayaks in white sealskins to look like icebergs. This brilliant camouflage allowed the Thule to approach a Viking village unseen. Their expansion across harsh territory was made possible by survival skills that enabled them to hunt and gather as they went. They depended upon no one.

Surprise Victory

It was 1260. The mighty Mongol army swept westward, demolishing everything in its way. Great cities such as Baghdad had fallen, and now the army wanted to tackle Egypt and the Mamluks. The Mongols thought their 20,000 soldiers would win easily. So they decided to face Mamluk Sultan Qutuz on the Plain of Esdraelon, in Palestine. But Qutuz hid most of his cavalry in the hills around the plain. The rest moved forward to lure the Mongols into battle. The Mongols charged confidently. Qutuz's hidden cavalry roared down onto the plain and defeated them. This famous victory was the Battle of Ain Jalut, meaning "Spring of Goliath."

More Ferocious Facts

- Young Aztec cadets became warriors once they had taken their first captive. They were now seen as men who were destined to die for the glory of the empire and return to Earth as hummingbirds.

- There were sometimes 20,000 soldiers in an Azande army. In spite of their numbers, they often planned an escape route. They attacked in the late afternoon so that they could disappear in the twilight.

- Queen Nanny (late 1600s–about 1733) was a fearsome leader of the Jamaican Maroons. It was said that she had supernatural powers that made her vanish into thin air. Her boiling cauldron was thought to suck in enemy soldiers.

- Sultan Baybars (1223–1277) was a very suspicious Mamluk ruler. He disguised himself during his soldiers' training to check that they were working hard enough. He also introduced a target game on horseback for them and built vast hippodromes in which they competed.

- The Azande's three-bladed *kpinga* knife was a perfect shock weapon. It weighed 3.5 lb (1.59 kg). The three blades were spread out so that if one blade missed its target, the next would hit it.

GLOSSARY

ASSASSIN
A killer who is usually hired for a particular target

BOSS
The humped center of a shield

CALTROP
A spiked metal weapon for gashing feet and hooves

CONCH
The shell of a large sea snail

DAIMYO
Japanese warlord

FEIGN
To pretend

GLADIUS
Roman sword

HIPPODROME
Arena for horse and chariot races

PILUM
Roman javelin

SHURIKEN
A pointed metal throwing weapon

SINEW
Tough, string-like tissue attaching a muscle to a bone

STOCKADE
Strong, tall wooden fence fortification

TERRAIN
Landscape—its shape, natural features, soil, and plant life

INDEX

THE AUTHOR

Catherine Chambers was born in Adelaide, South Australia, grew up in the UK, and studied African history and Swahili at the School of Oriental and African Studies in London. She has written about 130 books for children and young adults and enjoys seeking out intriguing facts for her nonfiction titles, which cover history, cultures, faiths, biography, geography, and the environment.

THE ILLUSTRATOR

Jason Juta is a South-African born illustrator living in London. He studied graphic design but turned to illustration, and now works in two styles. He creates fantasy art for the gaming industry (*Dungeons and Dragons* and *Star Wars*, for example), using 3-D to work out perspective, and personal work based on photography, with dark, mythic themes, painted in a traditional way.

Picture Credits (abbreviations: t = top; b = bottom; c = center; l = left; r = right)

© www.shutterstock.com: 6 bl, 6cr, 7tl